Castles

Simon Adams

WAYLAND

The History Detective Investigates series:
The Celts
Anglo-Saxons
Tudor Exploration
Tudor Home
Tudor Medicine
Tudor Theatre
Tudor War
The Civil Wars
Victorian Crime
Victorian Factory
Victorian School
Victorian Transport
Local History
The Industrial Revolution
Post-War Britain
The Normans and the Battle of Hastings
Monarchs
Weapons and Armour through the Ages
Castles

First published in 2010 by Wayland

This paperback edition published in 2012 by Wayland

Wayland
338 Euston Road
London NW1 3BH

Wayland Australia
Level 17/207 Kent Street
Sydney, NSW 2000

Editor: David John
Designer: Darren Jordan
Consultant: Andy Robertshaw

British Library Cataloguing in Publication Data:
Adams, Simon, 1955-
Castles. – (The history detective investigates)
1. Castles--History--Juvenile literature.
I. Title II. Series
728.8'1'09-dc22

ISBN: 978-0-7502-6949-0

Printed in China

Wayland is a division of Hachette Children's Books, an Hachette UK company

Picture Acknowledgments: Front cover top Christopher Rowlands/Dreamstime.com; front cover bottom Patti Gray/Dreamstime.com; 1 Gail Johnson/ Dreamstime.com; 2 Public Domain; 4 Karol Kozlowski/ Dreamstime.com; 5t David Hughes/Dreamstime. com; 5b Ira Block/Getty Images; 6 Dave Rudkin/ Getty Images; 7t Nitot/ShareAlike; 7b Max Homand/ iStockphoto.com; 8 Gail Johnson/Dreamstime.com; 9t Mark Bond/Dreamstime.com; 9b French School/ Getty Images; 10 Getty Images; 11t Public Domain; 11b Julien Trombini/Dreamstime.com; 12 iStockphoto. com; 13t Lyn Gateley/GNU; 13b Jacopo Robusti Tintoretto/Getty Images; 14 Public Domain; 15 Martinedegraaf/Dreamstime.com; 16 Geoff Dann/ Getty Images; 17t French School/Getty Images; 17b Patti Gray/Dreamstime.com; 18 National Geographic/ Getty Images; 19t Saladino/Dreamstime.com; 19b Dvkorn/Dreamstime.com; 20 Christopher Rowlands/ Dreamstime.com; 21t BridgetJones/Dreamstime.com; 21b Popperfoto/Getty Images; 22 Oosoom; 23t Eric Hill/GNU ShareAlike; 23b Dave Dunford; 24 French School/Getty Images; 25t Ryff, Walther Hermann/GNU ShareAlike; 25b Rafael Laguillo/Dreamstime.com; 26 Worldwide Picture Library/Alamy; 27t Softeis/GNU ShareAlike; 27b GNU/ShareAlike; 28 Gail Johnson/ Dreamstime.com; 29t Sean Gladwell/Dreamstime.com; 29b SuperStock/Getty Images.

Above: The coat of arms of the duke of Normandy features two leopards.
Previous page: Alnwick Castle in Northumberland, England, is often used as a film set today.

Contents

Words in **bold** can be found in the glossary on page 30.

The history detective Sherlock Bones will help you to find clues and collect evidence about castles. Wherever you see one of Sherlock's paw-prints, you will find a mystery to solve. The answers can be found on page 31.

What is a castle?

Castles are hugely impressive buildings, dominating the landscape and towering above the nearby houses. But what exactly is a castle, and what were castles built for?

A castle is a large, **fortified** military residence, usually built of stone. It had two main purposes. It was built for a ruler or a powerful **nobleman** or lord, his family, servants, **knights**, soldiers, and other people. It was also a military base where the lord could shelter from his enemies and give protection to local people during wars and from which he could ride out to attack his enemies. The first castles were built more than 1,000 years ago in Europe, but some also exist in Asia and Africa.

Castles are often confused with forts or fortresses, but they are quite different. A fort is a defensive military building or a larger fortified enclosure containing many buildings. Forts are built to withstand attack and keep the troops and other people inside safe. A large fort is known as a fortress.

Detective work

Are there any castles near where you live? Find out in your local library, or ask at the local tourist office. The castle will probably be ruined, but it will still give you a good idea of what it must have looked like when it was first built, hundreds of years ago.

Leeds Castle in Kent was largely built in the thirteenth century on the site of an earlier castle.

Chepstow Castle in Wales is one of the oldest surviving stone castles in Britain. Work started on the castle in 1067.

Armies build forts and fortresses to protect their troops or defend their country against attack. Towns were often surrounded by high walls for the same reason. The names castle and fort are often used for each other. Maiden Castle in southern England, for example, is not a stone castle but a hill fort. It was built of earth over 2,000 years ago, and consists of a series of earth mounds and ditches on top of a hill to protect a small town from attack.

Why did the inhabitants of Maiden Castle pick that site for their settlement?

In this book, we will look at the history of castles, from the first castles thrown up in France in the tenth century to the last, romantic castles of the nineteenth century. We will look at how these castles were built, what they were used for, and who lived there.

Maiden Castle in Dorset is the largest hill fort in Britain. Its ditches and mounds once enclosed a settlement.

What was a motte and bailey?

During the eighth century CE, a ruler called Charlemagne built up an empire in Europe that stretched from France to Germany and Italy. In the ninth century CE, these lands came under attack from raiding Vikings from Scandinavia, and Magyars from eastern Europe. To defend themselves, local rulers started to build castles.

At first these castles were nothing more than simple earth **ringworks** surrounded by a flooded ditch. Earth from digging the ditch was thrown up to form a **rampart**, or embankment, on top of which was a protective wooden **palisade**, or fence. In times of trouble, the lord, his family and soldiers sheltered behind the palisade from the attacking enemy.

In 1066, Duke William of Normandy invaded England and conquered the country. The new king – William I, 'the Conqueror' – needed to keep order among the hostile English. He brought with him a design for a complex form of castle that had been developed in Normandy. Known as a **motte and bailey**, it consisted of a courtyard (or **bailey**) surrounded by a palisade. This enclosed the living quarters, a main hall for eating, kitchens, stables and other buildings, and a well for fresh water.

Detective work

The Normans were the first people to build castles in England. Find out more about the Normans, who they were, where they came from, and why they conquered England at www.historyonthenet.com/Normans/normansmain.htm

What highly effective weapon could attackers use against wooden fortifications?

This model shows a motte and bailey castle, with the wooden tower and the bailey surrounded by palisades.

The Norman motte and bailey at Chateau de Gisors in northern France was built in about 1095. The stone tower on top of the motte was added a few years later.

'The richest and noblest of men ... in order to protect themselves from their enemies, and ... to subdue those weaker, of raising an earthen mound of the greatest possible height, cutting a wide ditch around it, fortifying its upper edge with square timbers tied together as in a wall, creating towers around it and building inside a house or citadel that dominates the whole structure.'

A French clergyman writing in the early 1000s about the first castles.

Next to the bailey stood a tall, earthen mound (or **motte**). This was up to 25 m (80 ft) high and built of layers of earth pressed tightly together. On top of the motte was a wooden tower surrounded by a palisade. In times of trouble, people left the bailey and fled up a **drawbridge** onto the motte, from where they could hurl down arrows and missiles at the attacking army below. A flooded **moat** or dry ditch surrounding the entire castle kept the enemy at a safe distance.

La Latte Castle was built in Brittany, France, in the thirteenth century. Perched over the sea on a narrow spit of land, it could only be entered by the drawbridge.

The Normans built motte and bailey castles by towns and on bends of rivers and other strategic sites. The advantage of this design was that it was quick and easy to build. Teams of soldiers and local labourers could make a castle in a couple of months. The Normans constructed at least 600 of them in the century after their invasion of 1066.

When was the first stone castle built?

Stone castles are not that easy to date. They do not have commemorative plaques on their walls stating when the first stone was laid, and there were no photographs from the opening ceremony. However, historians all agree that the first stone castles were built in northern France in the late tenth century.

The reason stone replaced earth and wood as the main building material was that it was stronger and made the castle less vulnerable to attack. Wooden castles were quite flimsy and easily destroyed by fire. Unlike motte and bailey castles, however, stone castles took years to build. It took **stonemasons** 10 to 15 years to build a tower, while a whole castle might not be finished for 25 years.

The first stone castles were built in England by the Normans. Chepstow Castle on the River Wye bordering Wales was begun in around 1067, Colchester Castle in Essex in around 1076, and the Tower of London (see pages 10–11) in 1078. Work also soon started at Rochester in Kent and Richmond in Yorkshire.

In the castle below, what defensive features did the stonemasons build into the walls?

The Norman tower at Cardiff Castle in Wales was built on a high motte in around 1081.

Work on the massive stone tower of Rochester Castle in Kent began in the late eleventh century.

Hundreds more stone castles followed over the next 500 years. Many of these new castles were built on the site of earlier motte and bailey or earthen ringwork castles, and made use of the motte on which to build a great stone tower, or **donjon**. At Restormel Castle in Cornwall, the wooden walls of the previous castle were simply replaced with stone.

The design of each castle varied according to its site and the stone used to build it. Basically, however, each castle consisted of a simple walled enclosure. A high **curtain wall** surrounded the site and protected the stables, kitchens and other buildings in the courtyard. At the centre stood a stone donjon that was roughly square, rectangular or cylindrical in shape. This tower housed the lord and his family and was heavily defended against attack. The donjon is sometimes wrongly called a keep.

Hundreds of stonemasons, carpenters, other craftsmen and labourers were needed to build an **enclosure castle**. The cost was immense. Henry II and his sons, Richard I and John, reigned from 1154 to 1216. Their total income from taxes and land rents was around £10,000 a year (£100 million in today's prices), of which £1,000 each year was spent building castles.

Detective work

Castle-building was a lengthy and laborious process. Find out more about the cost of building a castle, and the different materials and skills required, at www.castles-of-britain.com/castle88.htm

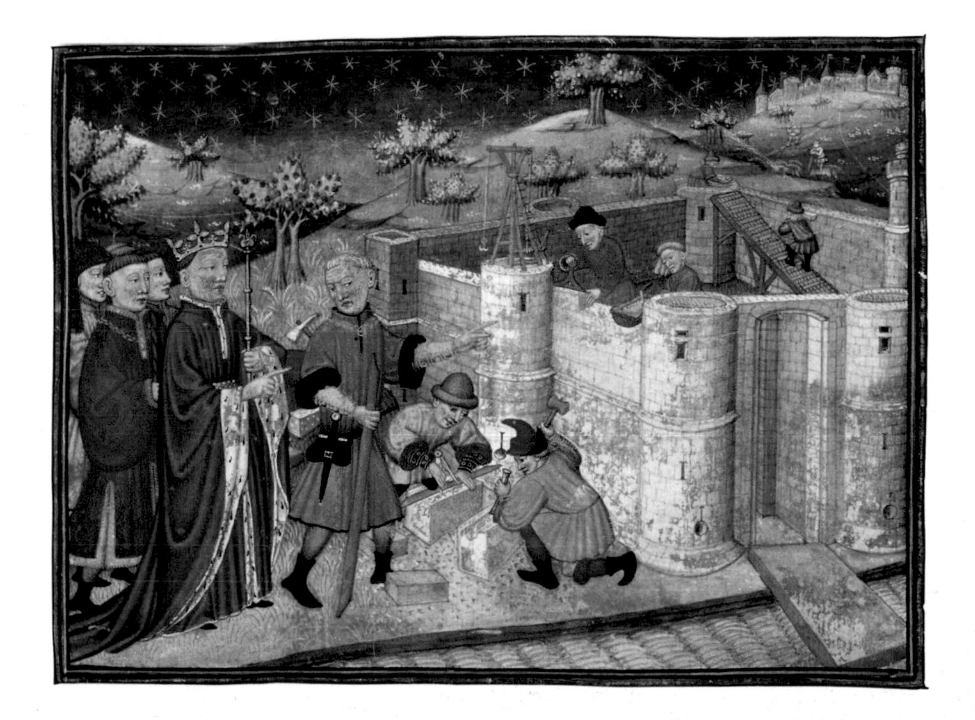

This medieval French illustration shows craftsmen at work on a stone castle. The castle is surrounded by a moat, which is crossed by a drawbridge.

Who built the Tower of London?

Millions of people visit the Tower of London every year to see the Crown Jewels. They also look at the Beefeater guards (the Yeoman Warders) in their distinctive red uniforms. But not many people realise that the Tower is actually London's very own castle.

A few months after his victory over the English at Hastings in 1066, William the Conqueror reached London. When he arrived there, he hastily erected a simple wooden castle by the River Thames. The castle was designed to show the people of London the power of their new king. In 1078, work started on the stone tower. The tower was completed in 1100. It is almost square in shape, and its thick walls rise 30 m (100 ft) to the **battlements** along the top. The tower was soon known as the White Tower because it was painted white.

DETECTIVE WORK

Today the Tower of London is not just a castle but a living monument to British history. Find out more about the Tower by visiting www.camelotintl.com/tower_site

The White Tower, built from 1078, stands within the walled enclosure of the Tower of London.

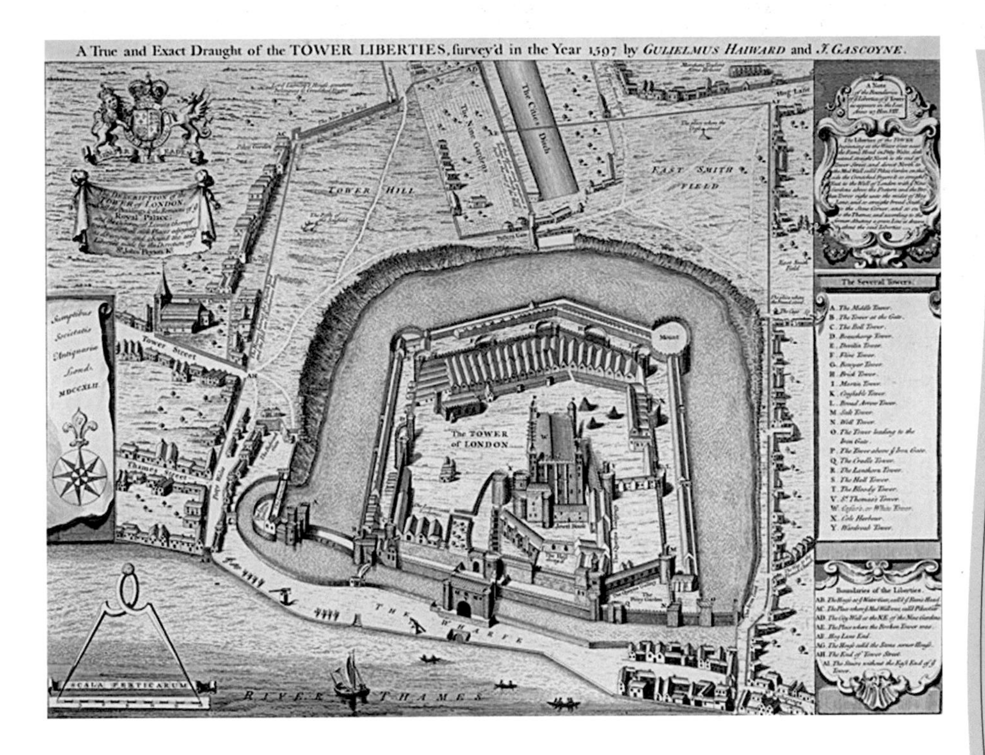

This drawing shows the Tower of London as it was in 1587, with its outer towers and wall, and the White Tower at the centre.

During the reign of Elizabeth I (1558–1603), the English historian John Stowe wrote that the Tower was:

'a citadel to defend or command the city, a royal palace for assemblies or treaties, a prison of state of the most dangerous offenders; the only place of coinage for all England … The armoury for warlike provision; the treasury of the ornaments and jewels of the crown; and general conservor of the most recent records of the queen's courts of justice.'

What is strange about the original entrance to the White Tower?

Over the next 200 years, English kings expanded the castle to form a large, stone-walled enclosure with many stone buildings inside. During the reign of Edward I (reigned 1272–1307), a second outer wall and three smaller towers were constructed. Over the next 600 years, a variety of residential, administrative and military buildings were constructed in the castle grounds.

The Tower of London has had many roles. It served as the main residence for English kings from William II (reigned 1086–1100) to Henry VII (reigned 1485–1509), and a place for them to retreat to in times of trouble. It also acted as royal prison. It is likely that Edward V and his brother Richard were both killed here by their uncle, Richard III, in 1483, and Anne Boleyn was imprisoned here before her execution by husband Henry VIII in 1536. The Tower has also served as an arsenal (weapons' store), the Royal Mint (where coins were manufactured), a royal zoo, and a safe place to store the Crown Jewels.

The White Tower is home to St John's Chapel, which was built in 1080.

Why were castles built in circles?

Caerphilly Castle in South Wales was the earliest concentric castle built in Britain.

During the 1200s, the design of castles in western Europe suddenly changed. The old design of a central square or rectangular tower surrounded by a single high wall was replaced by a new design with a concentric, or double, circle of walls and round towers.

The first stone castles were built with a single outer wall to stop attackers seizing the main tower. But if the attackers managed to get over or under the wall, either with ladders or by tunnelling, the castle was lost. A new design was needed to keep the enemy out. It was found in an unlikely place.

In 1095, Pope Urban II, head of the Roman Catholic Church, urged Christian warriors from Europe to go to the **Holy Land** to rid the holy places, such as Jerusalem, of their Muslim inhabitants. Thousands of **Crusaders**, as these warriors were known (see pages 18–19), answered his call. On their way to the Holy Land, the Crusaders passed through Constantinople (now Istanbul), capital of the Byzantine empire. There they saw that the city was surrounded by not one but two sets of walls set about 4.6 m (15 ft) apart.

How did the Crusaders scale the walls of Constantinople in 1204?

Both walls had numerous towers at regular intervals along their length. A deep moat surrounded the outer wall. These city walls had been constructed in the early 400s CE and withstood all attackers until the Crusaders themselves stormed Constantinople in 1204.

The Crusaders brought this concentric design back home with them and used it to build castles. Archers positioned on the taller inner wall could fire over the heads of those on the outer wall, doubling the rate of fire against an attacker. If that army managed to cross the moat and scale the outer wall, they still had the inner wall to tackle. The round towers were less easy to climb than square ones, while storming the castle through the heavily fortified **gatehouses** was almost impossible.

Construction of Beaumaris Castle, in Anglesey, North Wales, was begun in 1295. It was never completed as Edward I turned his attention towards Scotland instead.

The first concentric castle built in Britain was constructed at Caerphilly in South Wales after 1268. Further concentric castles were built in North Wales by Edward I (see pages 20–21), while many existing castles – including the Tower of London and Dover Castle – were altered so that they gained an additional outer wall and became concentric.

Detective work

Caerphilly Castle is one of the greatest castles in western Europe and the second largest in Britain after Windsor Castle. Find out more about its history and design at www.castlewales.com/caerphil.html

A painting by the great sixteenth-century Italian artist Tintoretto shows the capture of Constantinople in 1204 by the Crusaders.

Who lived inside a castle?

A castle was not just a fortified stronghold designed to keep attackers out. It was also a family house and home for many different types of people. So who lived inside a castle, and what did they all do?

The main occupant of a castle was its owner, the lord. The greatest and most powerful lord was the king himself, who owned many castles around the country and moved from one to another during the year. The lords ran large estates, or farms, around the castle. Along with the lord was his wife, the lady of the castle, who looked after it when the lord was away fighting. She entertained guests and looked after the lord's children.

The lord kept his own armed guard of knights, who lived in the castle with him. These mounted soldiers owed allegiance to the lord and served him in battle. In turn, they received accommodation and other rewards. Teenage squires who were training to be knights, and pages learning how to handle weapons and horses, also lived in the castle.

A fifteenth-century manuscript shows a duke's household exchanging New Year's gifts.

How did people keep the rooms warm and comfortable in medieval castles?

Peter of Blois, a courtier of Henry II, described the commotion that took place when the king was on the move from castle to castle:

'he is sure to upset all the arrangements by departing early in the morning. And then you see men dashing around as if they were mad, beating packhorses, running carts into one another – in short, giving a lively imitation of Hell. If, on the other hand, the king … sleeps until midday. Then you will see packhorses loaded and waiting, the carts prepared, the courtiers dozing, traders fretting, and everyone grumbling.'

The castle required a large number of workers to help it function properly. Cooks, bakers and servants prepared the food, baked the bread, stocked the wine cellar, and made ale, cider and other drinks. Farm workers kept the many sheep, pigs, goats and chickens that lived in the courtyard or in the grounds outside the castle. One worker looked after the beehives that provided honey. Stablemen and blacksmiths tended the horses, while the armourer maintained the weapons. Carpenters and stonemasons were on hand to maintain the castle.

A large castle would also house a resident priest or monk, who held services in the chapel. As the lord could probably not read or write, he would use the priest to write his letters or else employ a secretary or clerk, as well as a book-keeper to keep his accounts.

Some of these people, like the lord and his lady, had their own chambers at the top of the great tower, but most slept in the great hall or in rooms around the castle walls.

The fire in a castle's kitchen burned all year round. A boy called the 'turnspit' sat beside it, turning a handle to rotate the meat as it cooked.

How did people who lived in castles have fun?

Life in a castle was not all war and fighting. When the country was at peace, the inhabitants of a castle enjoyed themselves in many different ways. Much of their enjoyment, however, still had a military purpose and prepared them all for war.

On special occasions, the lord would throw a wonderful banquet in the great hall. The lord, his lady and guests were served a variety of delicious dishes, their contents depending on the season as there was no refrigeration in those days so only fresh food could be served. Attendants served the food, while the guests were serenaded by minstrels, or singers, and entertained by the court jester, a joker employed by the lord to make people laugh.

When there was no feast, the castle's inhabitants entertained themselves. Women did embroidery while both men and women played chess and other board games. Travelling musicians and storytellers sang songs and recited tales of romance and great adventure.

Medieval minstrels performed songs that told stories about real and imaginary events.

Detective work

Tournaments were the most effective war game ever devised, training and preparing knights for the wars they would have to fight. Discover more about these exciting events at www.castles.me.uk/medieval-tournaments.htm

Tournaments were not for the faint-hearted. The twelfth-century poet Bertrand de Born wrote of a knight that:

'once he has started fighting, no noble knight thinks of anything but breaking heads and arms.'

How did knights in a mêlée spot their team members among their competitors?

In good weather, the lord and his knights hunted wild boar, deer, rabbits and game birds, such as pheasants and partridges. They also flew hawks and falcons to catch small mammals and fished from rods and lines. Hunting was good practice for war, as it helped the hunters improve their riding and archery skills.

Feasts were an opportunity for entertainment and gossip.

The best practice for war, however, was the tournament. Teams of knights fought a mock battle known as a tourney or mêlée that took place over a large area of countryside. Groups of foot soldiers also took part to make the battle more realistic. The knights wore suits of armour and used real weapons, but during the 1200s, blunted weapons were introduced to reduce casualties. At much the same time, the joust was introduced. Two mounted knights charged each other with lances in order to knock the other off his horse.

Jousters used lances to knock each other off their horses.

Why did the Crusaders build castles?

The Crusading knights who went to seize the Holy Land after 1095 needed strongholds to protect themselves from Muslim warriors. As in Europe, these knights built castles.

On their way through the Byzantine empire, which occupied south-eastern Europe and western Turkey, the Crusaders were impressed by the strength of the local fortresses. Once in the Holy Land, they began to build their own castles based on this knowledge. These castles served as administrative centres for the new Crusader kingdoms, border posts commanding the major trade routes, and safe havens for **pilgrims** on their way to and from the holy places. These new castles were usually built by the sea or a river and had strong walls and deep ditches to protect their landward side. The castles had to be built fast, as the Crusaders were under attack from Muslim fighters, so were often just rectangular enclosures with a single main tower.

In 1095, Pope Urban II urged Europe to attack the Muslim inhabitants of the Holy Land. His words are not recorded, but it is reported that he said:

'I beseech you as Christ's heralds to publish this everywhere and to persuade all people of whatever rank, foot soldiers and knights, poor and rich, to carry aid promptly to those Christians and to destroy that vile race [the Muslims] from the lands of our friends. I say this to those who are present, it meant also for those who are absent. God wills it.'

This modern artwork shows Crusaders besieging Jerusalem in 1099.

The exception to this simple style is one of the most dramatic castles in the world. Krak des Chevaliers in Syria stands on the site of a former Muslim fortress on a hill above the River Orontes. As there was only one entrance to the castle, it was almost impossible to attack. The castle was built by the Knights Hospitaller after 1144. It has a basic concentric design, with the two sets of walls separated by a deep moat.

The castle's weakness was that it relied for its water supply on an **aqueduct** that brought water into the castle from the nearby hills. If the aqueduct were seized, the castle would soon run out of water. Muslim fighters repeatedly besieged the castle, but it was not taken until 1270, when an Egyptian army under Sultan Baybars cut off its water supply. The 200 knights inside held off the attackers for six weeks until Baybars and his troops managed to break in.

Detective work

In 1212, a large group of children set out to the Holy Land to achieve what the adults had failed to do in the four previous Crusades. Read about the remarkable and tragic Children's Crusade on www.historyguide.org/ancient/children.html

Krak des Chevaliers (above) was the mightiest Crusader fortress in the Holy Land.

The Knights Hospitaller (left) were Crusader knights. Their symbol was the cross of St John.

What features made Krak des Chevaliers so difficult to attack?

Why did Edward I build castles in Wales?

In 1272, Edward I came to the English throne. Edward was a warrior king, who was on Crusade in the Holy Land at the time and did not return to England until 1274. Once home, he was crowned king in Westminster Abbey and set out about unifying his new kingdom.

One of his first acts was to summon Prince Llywelyn Yr Ail of Wales to pay **homage** to him. At that time, central and northern Wales was a semi-independent **principality**, although its prince was meant to swear loyalty to the English king as his overlord. When Llywelyn refused to do this, Edward invaded the principality and defeated Llywelyn, forcing the homage from him. Five years later, Llywelyn rebelled again. With a large army, Edward invaded again, this time killing Llywelyn. In 1284, Wales was incorporated into England, ending its independence.

Despite the success of Edward's castles, the Welsh rose in revolt again in 1400. A clerk at the English court remarked that:

'The Welsh habit of revolt against the English is a long-standing madness ... from the sayings of the prophet Merlin they still hope to recover England.'

Conwy Castle was built in just four years, between 1283 and 1287, using 1,500 stonemasons and other workers.

DETECTIVE WORK

You can find out more about the castles Edward built in Wales, and some of the other 400 castles in the principality, by visiting www.castlewales.com/home.html

Caernarfon Castle was built by the side of the River Seiont in North Wales.

To make sure there was no Welsh rebellion again, Edward decided to build a string of castles across northern Wales. Ten new castles were built, the most famous of which are at Caernarfon, Conwy, Flint and Harlech. The scale of this building programme was immense: £80,000 was spent from 1277 to 1304 (at least £800 million in today's prices).

Vast teams of labourers were brought from around England, along with local people forced to work for the English. In 1286, 22 carpenters, 30 blacksmiths, 115 quarrymen, 227 stonemasons and 546 labourers were at work on Harlech Castle alone. Four of the castles were concentric in design, while the rest had a more traditional enclosure design with either towers along the outer wall or a large, central tower inside.

These castles were built to intimidate the Welsh. Large **garrisons** of English troops were stationed in them, along with administrators brought in to run the country. Five of the castles were built next to towns that were also fortified, creating English-speaking communities inside Welsh-speaking Wales. It was an extraordinarily powerful project that changed the face and politics of Wales forever.

King Edward I of England (reigned 1272–1307) built a series of impressive castles in Wales. In 1284, his son, the future Edward II, was born in Caernarfon Castle.

At what strategic locations were castles often built?

Did castles have architects?

When we learn about a castle, we usually know about the king in whose reign it was built. The Tower of London was started while William the Conqueror was on the throne, for example. But we have no names of those who actually designed or built the castle. In the case of the Welsh castles, however, we do have an architect's name, Master James of St Georges. But who was he, and where was he from?

One man was determined to find out about Master James. From 1946 to 1955 Arnold Taylor was Chief Inspector of Welsh Monuments. Part of his job was to look after the castles Edward I built in Wales. He knew that in 1278 Master James had arrived at Flint and Rhuddlan Castles 'to ordain the works of the castles there'. Master James then became 'Master of the King's Works in Wales' and was given a daily salary. Taylor studied the Master's castles and noticed that they had several unique features. The windows at Harlech were very large, while the design of the garderobes, or toilets – an important part of any castle – was unknown in other English or Welsh castles. Whoever this man was, he was not English.

Master James often had to beg for money from Edward I to finish his work. Writing from Beaumaris Castle, he said:

'In case you should wonder where so much money could go in a week, we would have you know that we have needed – 400 masons, both cutters and layers, together with 2,000 less skilled workmen ... 200 quarrymen; 30 smiths; and carpenters for putting in the joists and floor boards ... The men's pay has been and still is very much in arrears, and we are having the greatest difficulty in keeping them because they simply have nothing to live on.'

Harlech Castle commands wide views – far enough to see any approaching army.

Chillon Castle was home to the counts of Savoy.

Taylor decided to hunt for Master James in Savoy. Today this region is shared between France, Italy and Switzerland, but in the late 1300s it was an independent country, which had strong ties with England. Taylor knew that Edward I had stopped in Savoy on his way back to England from the Crusades in 1273. Taylor therefore went to Savoy to look at its castles. At Chillon Castle on Lake Geneva, he found the same design of windows as at Harlech, while at La Batiaz he found identical garderobes. When he checked Savoy's records, he discovered that their castles were built by a father and son team called Master John and Master James. One record shows Master James working on a castle in Lyon that Edward visited in 1273.

Arnold Taylor had found his man. Thanks to his efforts, we now know the name and life story of one of the most remarkable architects of all time. Master James was a man who so impressed Edward that he summoned him to Wales and put him in charge of building ten castles. These castles are almost unique in having an architect whose name and life story we know today.

What happened to the sewage that went into a castle's garderobe?

Garderobe towers were designed to stick out from the walls of a castle and housed the toilets.

Why were castles besieged?

Castles were designed to keep an enemy army out. They were built to be strong, with moats of water and steep ramparts of earth around them, one or two enclosing high walls, a drawbridge that was lifted up in times of danger, and towers and battlements from which soldiers could rain down missiles on the enemy below. So how did an enemy army capture a castle?

Planning a siege required time, men and effort. An attacking army would first surround a castle and stop supplies getting in and out, hoping to starve the castle into surrender. A message would be sent to the owner of the castle demanding that he surrender. If he refused, the siege began.

Attacking sappers (miners) dug tunnels under the castle walls, hoping to enter the courtyard. Sometimes they lit a fire in the tunnel to bring the walls above tumbling down. Catapults and **trebuchets** hurled rocks and burning missiles, and **ballistas** that fired metal bolts, aimed to break through the walls or knock defending troops off the walls. A battering ram was used to smash the main gate. Soldiers also wheeled up a siege tower – a tower of ladders as high as the castle wall – that allowed attacking troops hidden inside to climb over the top of the wall.

A Turkish army is surrounding a Crusader castle. The men are winding crossbows ready to shoot metal bolts at the knights on the walls.

This medieval drawing shows an army destroying a castle's walls with battering rams.

DETECTIVE WORK

A siege was a lengthy affair, with a lot of specialist equipment involved. Read more about how a siege was organised and how some of these siege engines worked, on www.siege-engine.com

As the siege progressed, the soldiers inside the castle defended it as best they could. Troops along the battlements kept up a steady fire of missiles against the enemy. Walls were repaired if they were damaged and a watch was kept for any signs of tunnelling.

How are the men besieging the walls in the drawing (left) protecting themselves from missiles?

Starvation, a loss of will to continue fighting, or the forced entry of the enemy into the castle, eventually brought the siege to an end after months or even years. The castle was now in the enemy's hands. Sometimes everyone inside was killed, but more often the lord and his knights were captured and held to ransom, or held until a large fee was paid for their release.

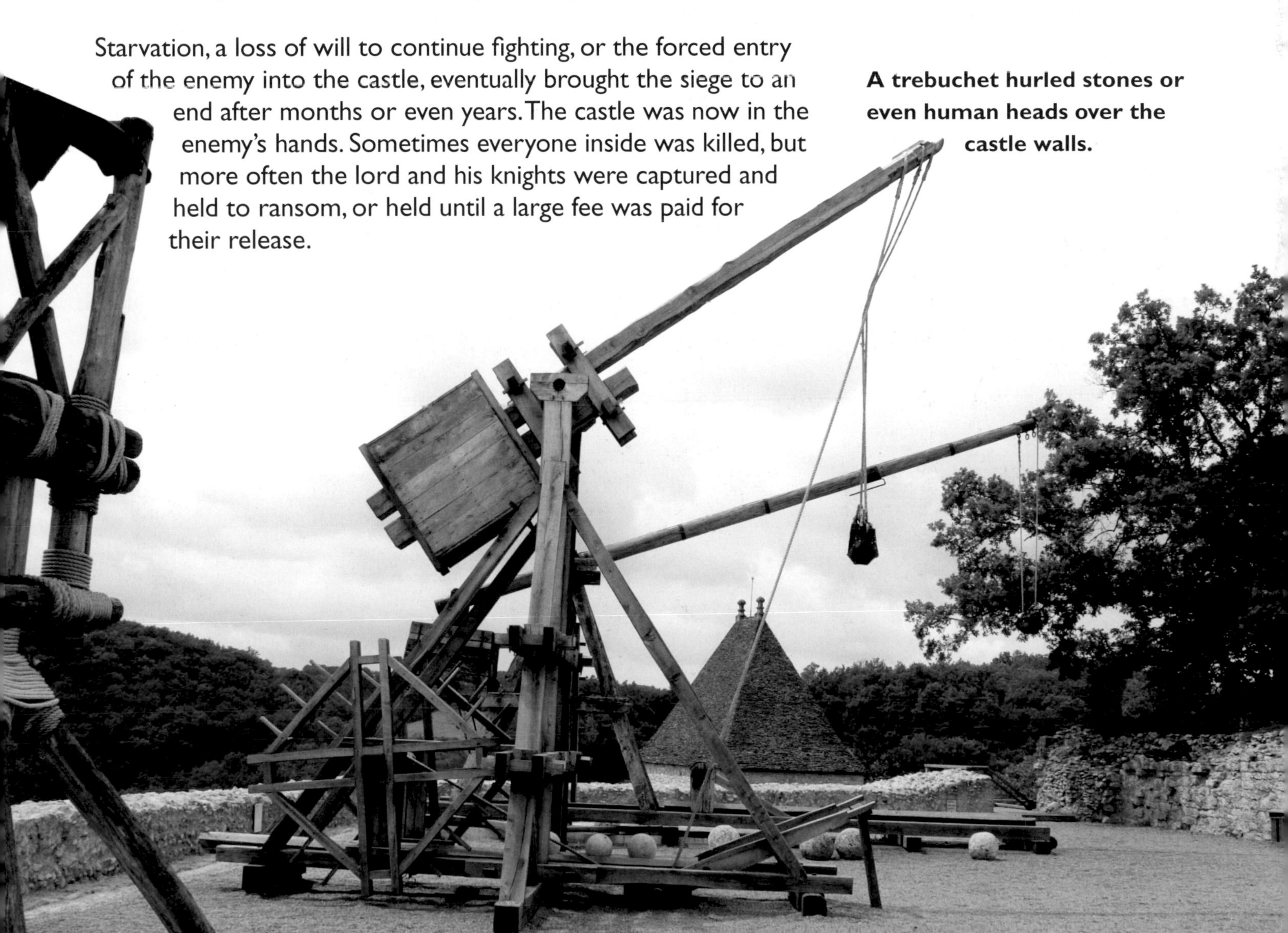

A trebuchet hurled stones or even human heads over the castle walls.

Why did castle-building stop?

The castles we see around us today are at least 500 years old and most are in ruins. Few are now lived in or used for protection. So when did castle-building stop, and why?

Castles were first built at a time of great chaos in Europe. There were no strong, central governments to protect a country from enemy armies, and powerful local lords fought each other for control of their lands. Castles were vital to protect people and to control a region or province. By the late 1400s, however, castles had begun to lose their military importance. Strong kings in England, France and elsewhere brought peace to their countries and often forbade their nobles from building new castles. Society became more stable and life less brutal. Most importantly, the introduction of gunpowder into western Europe in the early 1300s slowly changed the way wars were fought. Strong cannon could blast through a castle wall, making a castle easier to capture.

This medieval supergun, known as 'Mons Meg', was made in 1449 and given as a gift to King James II of Scotland. It fired balls that weighed 180 kg (400 lb).

In 1868 King Ludwig II of Bavaria wrote to his friend, the composer Richard Wagner:

'I intend to rebuild the old castle ruins of Hohenschwangau by the Pöllat gorge in the genuine style of the old German knightly fortresses... the location is the most beautiful one could find, holy and unapproachable'

The castle, known as Neuschwanstein, took 23 years to build but was never finished. The king spent just 11 nights in his dream castle in 1884.

Neuschwanstein in Bavaria, Germany, is the most spectacular of the nineteenth-century castles. It was more comfortable than a medieval castle, with modern plumbing and electric lights.

As a result, castles became less important. Some were turned into army barracks while many became homes. Most were left to collapse, and their stones were taken for new buildings. A few new castles were still built in lawless areas, such as Scotland, where fortified tower-houses protected families from raiders. By the 1700s, the age of the castle was over.

During the nineteenth century, however, people became interested in castles once more. In the kingdom of Bavaria in southern Germany, King Ludwig II began work on the fairytale castle of Neuschwanstein. It stands on a high rocky crag, but despite its towers, **turrets** and battlements it had no military function and was purely an eccentric man's dream. Other rich men built mock castles known as follies in which they could pretend they lived at a time when knights in shining armour rode around the countryside, and lords and their ladies held banquets in the castle's great hall. But these were just dreams. In reality, castles were now part of history.

Carrigafoyle Castle in Ireland was destroyed by siege cannon in 1580.

Your project

By now you should have collected lots of information about castles and their fascinating history. This is the time to think about the sort of project you might like to produce.

You could choose your favourite castle and write its history from its beginnings to the present day. What are the interesting parts of the castle's history? Think of the time when it was being built, or later under siege. Or write instead about what it was like to live and work inside a castle, as a lord or lady, or as a knight or a common soldier or cook. What sort of life did they lead, what clothes would they wear, what food and drink would they have?

Alternatively, you could try to design your own castle. Where would you put the walls and great tower, and how many people would you need to dig the moat? You might find this website of use: http://score.rims.k12.ca.us/activity/castle_builder/

You might have your own ideas for a project, but whatever you decide, remember it is your project, so choose something that interests you. Good luck!

Alnwick Castle in Northumberland was begun by the Normans in 1096. It is still in use today, as the home of the duke of Northumberland.

Project presentation

- Research your project well. Use the Internet and your local or school library. Is there a nearby society, museum or historical site related to your project? Many of these will also have their own Internet site. Is there a castle in your own area you could research?

- If you were a time-travelling journalist and could go back to when a castle was in full use, what questions would you ask the people in it? Make a list, then see if you can answer those questions from your research.

- Collect pictures about your subject and use them to illustrate your research. You could also compile a list of useful websites and other sources of information.

Some castles still have their original portcullis. This was a heavy grille that dropped down to bar entry into the castle courtyard.

Medieval illustrations often show the busy life of a castle, with servants at work and the lord and lady feasting or engaging in other pastimes.

Glossary

aqueduct A stone or brick channel that brings water from a river into a castle or other building or town.

bailey A castle courtyard. Also called a ward.

ballista A siege engine that used a twisted rope that, when suddenly released, fired a large metal bolt.

battlement The parapet of a wall with openings, known as crenelles, through which archers fired their weapons.

CE 'Common Era'. Used to signify years since the believed birth of Jesus.

Crusader A person who went from Europe on one of the Crusades, or military campaigns, between 1095 and 1291 to seize control of the Holy Land from its Muslim inhabitants.

curtain wall A general term for a castle wall that surrounded a courtyard. This wall got its name because it often appeared to be hung between towers or between a tower and the gatehouse.

donjon The great tower of a castle.

drawbridge A bridge over a moat or ditch that could be lifted to prevent an enemy entering a castle.

enclosure castle A castle with a single outer wall.

fortification A fortified military building.

fortified Strengthened.

garrison A group of soldiers stationed in a place such as a castle, town or fort.

gatehouse The fortified entrance to the castle housing the drawbridge.

Holy Land The area of modern-day Syria, Israel and Lebanon, where events described in the Bible took place.

homage The public display of loyalty to a king or master.

knight A mounted, heavily armed soldier.

moat A flooded ditch surrounding a castle.

motte A defensive mound built with layers of earth.

motte and bailey An early type of castle consisting of a fortified mound and courtyard, surrounded by a moat.

nobleman A high-ranking lord or other titled man who owned and controlled large estates of land.

palisade A strong wooden fence used to defend a castle.

pilgrim A religious person who makes a journey to a holy place.

principality A country ruled by a prince.

rampart An earthen embankment surrounding a castle or forming part of a ringwork.

ringwork A roughly circular earthen defensive structure consisting of ramparts and ditches.

stonemason A craftsman who worked in stone. Often called a mason.

trebuchet A siege engine with a pivoting wooden arm from which a large rock could be released.

turret A small tower that projects from the wall of a castle.

Answers

Page 5: It was on a hill, which gave the inhabitants good views over the surrounding area and would make it easier to defend in case of an attack.

Page 6: Attackers could use fire, either carried by flaming torches or by burning arrows or other missiles shot into the wooden fortifications.

Page 8: They built battlements at the top of the walls, through which archers could fire their weapons, as well as narrow arrow slits in the walls, which served the same purpose.

Page 11: It is at first-floor level and is reached only by a removable wooden staircase.

Page 12: They sailed their ships close to the sea wall and pushed ladders up to the towers.

Page 14: Many rooms had fireplaces in which fires could be built for warmth, and wall hangings could keep out the draughts from windows.

Page 16: Each team wore a different design, known as a coat of arms, on their clothes and shields.

Page 19: It is on a steep hill, has access only via a drawbridge, and has very thick walls to protect against bombardment.

Page 21: Castles were often built to guard rivers, as well as roads and coastlines.

Page 23: It fell into a pit or the castle's moat.

Page 25: Some of the battering rams have roofs to protect the men pushing the ram.

Further Information

Books to read

Castles and Forts by Simon Adams (Kingfisher 2003)
Eyewitness Castle by Christopher Gravett (Dorling Kindersley 1994)
Castle by Marc Morris (Macmillan 2003)
Castles by Plantagenet Somerset Fry (David & Charles 2008)

Websites

www.castles.org
www.castlewales.com/home.html
www.castlexplorer.co.uk

Note to parents and teachers: Every effort has been made by the publishers to ensure that these websites are suitable for children. However, because of the nature of the Internet, it is impossible to guarantee that the contents of these sites will not be altered. We strongly advise that Internet access is supervised by a responsible adult.

Places to visit

There are more than 1,300 castles to visit in Britain and Ireland. Among the most spectacular are:
The Tower of London, London EC3N 4AB
Caerphilly Castle, Caerphilly CF83 1NZ
Edinburgh Castle, Edinburgh EH1 2NG
Carrickfergus Castle, Carrickfergus BT38 7BG

Index

Numbers in **bold** refer to pictures and captions